C000262816

THE ORVIS STREAMSIDE GUIDE TO
Fly Casting

THE ORVIS STREAMSIDE GUIDE TO
Fly Casting

TOM DECK

Illustrations by Rod Walinchus
Photographs by Tom Rosenbauer

The Lyons Press

This book is dedicated to
Julie, Donny, Debbie, Michael, Freddie,
and to Mom and Dad

Copyright © 2000 by Tom Deck

Illustrations by Rod Walinchus

10 9 8 7 6 5 4 3 2 1

Printed in China

              Library of Congress Cataloging-in-Publication Data
Deck, Tom.
    The Orvis streamside guide to fly casting / Tom Deck; illustrations
by Rod Walinchus.
        p.   cm.
    ISBN 1-55821-987-0
    1. Fly casting.   I. Title.

  SH454.2 .D43 1999
  799.1´24—dc21
                                                              99-047874

CONTENTS

ACKNOWLEDGMENTS

I would like to thank Tom Rosenbauer for all the sound advice and for giving me an opportunity. I would also like to thank Jay Cassell. Thanks to all my peers and mentors at the Orvis Fly-Fishing Schools and to Dickie Davis for always catching the fish. Lastly, thanks to Trina Sabin for her patience and support.

FOREWORD

Much has happened in fly casting since I wrote the casting section of *The Orvis Fly-Fishing Guide* back in 1984. Schools have blossomed all over the country, and you can now learn fly casting in locales as varied as the Florida Keys, the sand flats of Cape Cod, or the chalk streams of southern England. Video technology was in its infancy back then, but we now have scores of good casting tapes and CD-ROMs. You can even get casting tips over the Internet. All of these methods are better than learning from a book, but casting books still have their place. You can't refer to a video when you have a problem that needs correcting in the middle of the river, and you can't get casting tips while reading on an airplane. Books are concise, don't require additional technology, and are affordable.

This book is not the definitive casting book for every tricky variation of the overhead cast. It is meant to be a reference guide for novice and intermediate casters, where quick answers can be found without wading through a lot on information you'll never use. It's a book to refer to after attending a fishing school or studying a videotape.

Fly-casting instructions cannot be archived like a database. Casting tips make up more of an oral history, and this one follows America's longest-running fly-casting school. Tens of thousands of students have attended the Orvis schools since Bill Cairns began them in 1968. The Orvis method as originally taught by Bill Cairns was refined by the late Tony Skilton, then by Rick Rishell, and finally by Tom Deck, the author of this book. The Orvis Progressive Method is not one man's opinion of how fly casting should be taught, which is what you will find in other casting books. It is an empirical distillation of what has worked for students since 1968. There is nothing here that has not been refined without the input of thousands of students and scores of different instructors.

In my five years of instruction in the Orvis schools, I saw very few people who could pick up fly casting in a few hours. Fran Tarkenton, the great quarterback of the Vikings and Giants, picked it up as quickly as anyone I have ever seen, but how many of us can claim his hand-eye coordination? Even those people considered to be great fly casters are never satisfied with their skill, so they practice almost every day. Heck, there have been scores of physicists who have studied fly casting, and none of them even agree on why it works!

Practice on your front lawn. Practice in a back alley in Manhattan or San Francisco on your lunch hour. Practice when you're on the water and fishing is slow. Try to improve a little every time you pick up a rod. When you run into trouble, take this book out of your pocket and let Tom's advice smooth out the wrinkles.

TOM ROSENBAUER

PART ONE

THE FUNDAMENTALS

GOAL: To effectively control the size of your casting loop and to be able to pick up and lay down 20 to 30 feet of line so that it straightens completely just above the water.

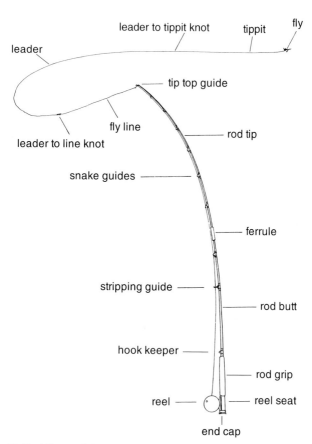

Fly Rod Nomenclature

CHAPTER 1

GRIP AND STANCE

THE CORRECT GRIP

The way you hold the rod is extremely important. The grip is your connection to the rod, and if you have a good connection, it will help your cast tremendously. Proper grip is often neglected, as many people tend to focus solely on the path of the rod tip during the casting stroke.

There are two grip variations worth exploring. The first grip option is to place the index finger on top of the cork grip (see illustration on page 4). This is especially helpful for beginners who have trouble developing the proper backcast position. It is very hard to force the index finger to go too far backward in the casting stroke. Try it! This grip creates a sense of pointing rather than casting, and most new fly rodders can point the tip of the rod much easier than they can cast it.

The index-finger grip is preferred when using lighter lines and especially when casting short, soft rods. This grip is a favored any time the rod length is shorter than 7½ feet. The index-finger grip has its place with certain rods and in certain situations, but it also has its limitations. This grip does not use the stronger muscles of the casting arm and it can become fatiguing if you are casting heavier, longer rods over even a short period of time.

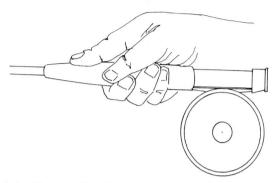

The Index Finger-on-Top Grip
This grip is preferred when using short, soft rods and lighter line weights. Beginners like it because it creates a sense of pointing rather than casting.

The second grip, which is used in most casting situations, is the thumb-on-top grip (see illustration on page 5). The thumb-on-top grip provides a better connection between the rod and the major casting muscles of the forearm and wrist. By placing the thumb on top, you can exert more pressure throughout the rod. That is why this grip is used more often with heavier lines and longer rods.

There is a little more to this grip than simply placing the thumb on top of the cork. Don't hold the rod with your thumb on top of the grip so there are no spaces between your fingers, as if you were hitchhiking. The rod should lay diagonally across your palm. With the correct grip, the rod butt should extend beyond your

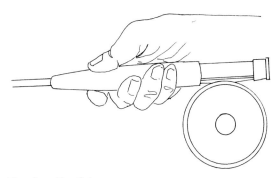

The Thumb-on-Top Grip
This is the best grip for all types of fishing situations.

palm and be just about parallel with your forearm. Hold onto the grip as if it were a hammer and you have just driven a nail home with the tip of the rod. The angle of this grip will allow you to maximize the strength of your forearm, and will let your wrist spring into play just when you need it.

Try this simple test to see which grip provides a better connection to the rod: Place the butt section of the rod in the palm of your left hand so that it is just below the stripping, or first guide. Place the thin end of the butt section on a table. Now, using the index-finger grip, try to put a slight bend in the rod. Next, try using your thumb-on-top grip, and put pressure on the palm of your hand. You should be able to exert more pressure and bend the rod slightly more with the latter grip.

No matter which grip you choose, it is important to hold the rod comfortably. The grip should become progressively firmer throughout the casting stroke, but should be relaxed when the rod is not in motion. By loosening the grip in between casting strokes, your hand will naturally dampen vibrations in the rod. This will make the line go farther and improve your presentation. Veins should not be bulging out of your forearm as you hold the rod. Relax your grip. This will allow you to fish comfortably for a longer time.

Improving your grip will not only connect you to the rod properly, it just might help you to connect to more fish as well!

STANCE

Most fishermen rarely think about foot placement or stance. Most of the time you're just trying to avoid falling into the water. But proper stance is important, because it will allow you to rotate your upper body and give you a greater range of motion. The correct foot placement for a right-hander is to lead with the left foot, so it is pointing straight ahead, in the direction of the cast. The right foot should be pulled back so that your stance is open. Image that your left foot is pointing directly at 12 o'clock. Your right foot should slide back and point somewhere between 2 and 3 o'clock. The right foot can point more toward 2 o'clock for shorter casts. For longer casts, which require a greater range of motion, pull the right foot

An open stance allows you to turn your head and see the position of the rod during the backcast.

a little farther back and aim it more toward 3 o'clock. An open stance allows you to turn your head and see the position of the rod and line during the backcast (see illustration on page 7).

Proper foot placement is critical, and I will refer to it again. Also remember that your stance should not be too wide or too narrow. Your feet should be spaced so that the rest of your body feels comfortably in balance.

CHAPTER 2

DEFINING THE CASTING ARC

The casting arc is the distance the rod travels throughout the casting stroke. If you can control the distance and shape of this arc, your overall fly casting will be greatly improved.

One of the most frequently used descriptions of the fly-casting arc is the old **clock method.** It has been immortalized in books and even in movies. If 12 o'clock is vertical (straight up), then according to the clock method, the rod should travel from 10 o'clock out in front to 2 o'clock behind (see illustration on page 10). This description, though accurate, is somewhat incomplete for fly-casting instruction.

First of all, the size of the arc is dictated by the amount of line that you are casting. The shorter the line you are casting, the less distance the rod tip travels. Conversely, the longer the cast, the farther the tip must travel through the casting arc. The casting arc is ever changing: As fishing conditions change, so does the path of the rod.

Let's start with shorter casts, which require less rod movement because shorter lengths of line require less energy to drive them through the air. When you are casting shorter distances, the rod will not bend or flex greatly—in fact, just the tip of the rod will flex (see illustration on page 11). New fly casters often want to wave their hand back and forth excessively, which will

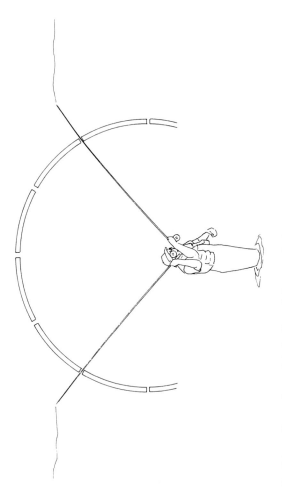

Don't learn fly casting solely by the points on a clock
The "clock method" is rigid and somewhat incomplete for fly-casting instruction. The casting arc is not set in stone from 10 o'clock to 2 o'clock. The size of the arc changes according to the length of line you are casting.

Short Cast / Smaller Casting Arc
Casting a shorter length of line requires less energy from the rod. There is often enough flex in just the tip of the rod to lay out a shorter cast.

move the rod tip too far back and too far forward. The key is that rod movement should be minimized when casting shorter distances. Less is in fact more.

To cast longer distances, your casting arc must progressively increase in size. If you want to cast more line, you must put more energy into the rod, and that comes from bending or flexing the rod. The more dis-

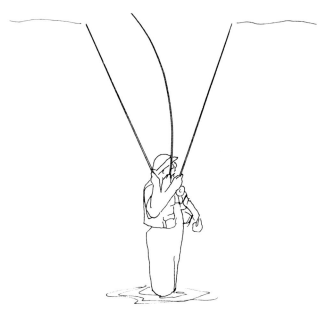

Medium Distance Cast / Medium Casting Arc
As the range of your casting increases, so does the casting arc; the flex extends down to the middle of the rod.

tance you want. the more the rod must flex during the casting stroke, which means you must increase the size of the casting arc. For medium-distance casts of 30 to 40 feet, in other words, the size of the arc will increase and the rod tip will travel further, through a longer casting stroke. The rod flex will also extend down into the middle section of the rod. More flex will translate into greater line speed and distance.

For your longest casts, the arc must open up even more and the flex must extend all the way down into the butt section of the fly rod. The butt section is the stiffest part of the rod, and it will hold the most energy. If you want to lay out a nice long line, you need to harness that energy.

Another point to be aware of is that the arc in fly casting can tilt slightly forward or backward. Tilting the arc backwards may be used to help shoot more line on the front cast when the wind is at your back, for

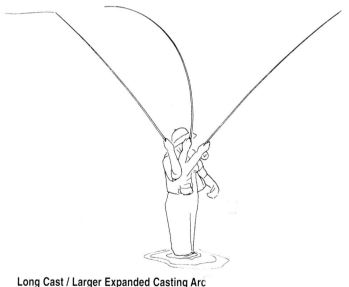

Long Cast / Larger Expanded Casting Arc
Long casts require that the rod travel through an expanded casting arc, which will allow it to bend all the way down to the butt section.

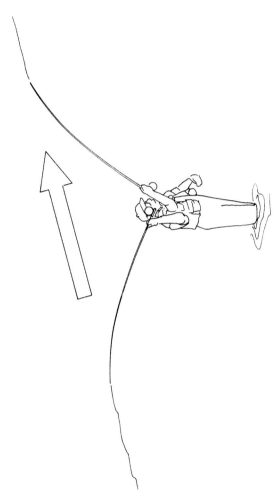

The casting arc may have to tilt backwards in order to shoot more line on the forward stroke. This is not advised for beginners trying to learn the basics.

14

The casting arc may be tilted forward in order to propel the backcast higher and the forward cast lower. This can be very effective when casting directly into the wind.

example. You can also adjust the angle of the casting arc forward by lowering the front cast (bringing the rod tip closer to the water) and stopping the rod vertically, at about 12 o'clock on the backcast. This will effectively propel the line up and back rather than behind you, which can be helpful for elevating line up over trees or shrubs that would otherwise be in the path of a conventional backcast stroke. Shortening the backcast and lowering the front cast can also help when you are casting into a head wind (see illustration on page 15). It will decrease the amount of hang time the line has over the water at the completion of the forward cast, which in turn will prevent the wind from blowing your presentation off its mark.

Adjust the angle and size of your casting arc for the amount of line you are handling. It will make your casting stroke smoother and more consistent.

CHAPTER 3

CASTING LOOPS

The size of the casting arc is critical, but the path the rod tip travels through the casting stroke is just as important, if not *more* important. Your casting arc may be the proper size, but if the track or path of your casting stroke is incorrect, the line will not straighten out completely. It is important to note that the rod tip dictates where the line will go. If the rod tip travels in a straight line throughout the casting stroke, you will have a perfect straight-line cast. The path the rod tip travels also determines the size of the casting loop.

A nice cast with a classic candy-cane-shaped loop.

17

What does a correct casting loop look like? If fly line had stripes on it, then good fly-casting loops would look like candy canes. As a rule, the smaller or narrower the loop at the end of the candy cane, the better (see illustration). Narrow loops tend to fly or cut through the air better than larger, more open loops.

First let me describe what *not* to do, because if you can avoid the negative you can then focus on what the correct rod path should be. At the Orvis Fly-Fishing School I have had the benefit of critiquing hundreds of fly casters on video. Most of the problems beginning fly rodders have stem from the trouble they have controlling the path of the rod.

The one problem I see most often is what I call the "igloo cast." Pretend that the rod tip has a paintbrush on it. If the paintbrush moves in a semicircular path overhead, as if you were painting the ceiling of an igloo, you will have extremely open casting loops and the fly line can not unfurl completely. Most new fly casters tend to drop the backcast too far back and drive their front cast too far forward (see illustration on page 20). Some beginning fly casters may have a proper backcast position, but they paint the ceiling of an igloo on the forward stroke. An interesting fact to note is that one can have the correct size casting arc, but if the tip of the rod moves in this "igloo-cast" fashion, the fly cast will still falter. Avoid painting the ceiling of an igloo at all costs.

The size of your fly-casting loops is determined by the way you stop the rod. There is very little follow-through in fly casting, especially when dealing with a

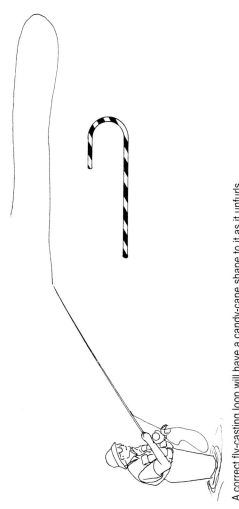

A correct fly-casting loop will have a candy-cane shape to it as it unfurls.

19

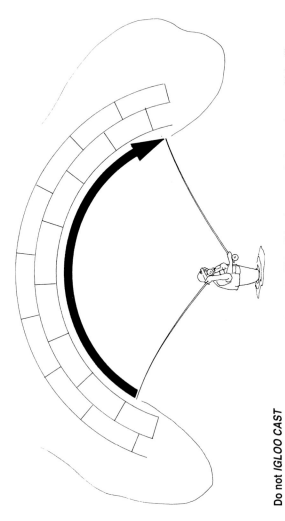

Do not *IGLOO CAST*
Avoid painting the ceiling of an igloo with the rod tip. This will lead to excessively open loops, which will cause the fly cast to falter.

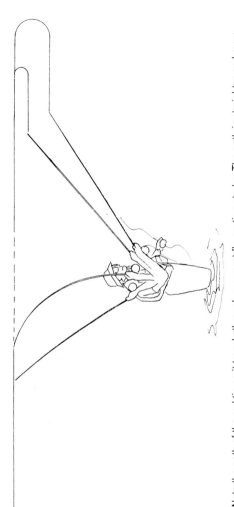

Note the path of the rod tip as it travels through a correct fly-casting stroke. The path is straighter and more direct. This is the opposite of the "igloo cast."

1. A narrow casting loop is formed by stopping the rod tip cleanly below the path of the fly line.

2. An open loop is caused by stopping the rod tip farther below the path of the fly line.

shorter length of fly line. You must smoothly bring the rod to an abrupt stop at the finish of each casting stroke. This is difficult for most people to do. In sports that have an arcing swing, such as golf or tennis, follow-through helps. In fly casting, too much follow-through causes loops to open up. Once the rod tip passes over the grip, the casting loop has been formed. The rod tip must tilt and drop a little below the flight path of the fly line. If it does not, the line will run into itself. Open loops are caused by excessively pulling or pointing the rod tip downward and failing to stop the rod decisively at the end of the cast. Remember, if you "igloo cast" just a little at either end of the casting arc, your loops will be too large and too open.

By drawing the rod tip in a straighter, more direct path, and driving it to a complete stop, your loops will become narrower. Stop the rod tip quickly after it has traveled over the casting hand, and you will have nice, tight casting loops that will cut through the air and travel more efficiently (see illustration on page 21).

Whether you are casting 20 feet of line with a narrow casting arc or laying out 50 feet with an expanded arc, the rod tip must stop cleanly just below the path of the fly line.

CHAPTER 4

THE PICK UP-AND-LAY DOWN CAST

The pick up-and-lay down cast has three primary parts: the pickup, the backcast, and the front cast. This is the first and most important cast in the Orvis Progressive Casting Method. Mastering this stroke will allow a caster to progress rapidly, building upon solid fundamentals. If you are a beginner, practicing this cast will help you develop your casting stroke. However, this cast is not only for beginners: It's perfect for correcting bad habits, because it can reprogram your muscle memory in a better way. If you are an accomplished caster, this cast may help you develop a feel and timing for a new rod.

The goal of the pick up-and-lay down cast is to have the line straighten out entirely above the surface of the water, then touch down quietly. The pick up-and-lay down drill is actually made up of two casts: First is the backcast, which will project the line up and back; then a front cast, which will lay the line out over the water. Both the front and backcasts are equally important, and must work together for your cast to succeed. The backcast is critical, because the way you project the line behind you in turn dictates how well the front cast will lay out in front of you.

Getting Started

You cannot start casting with just a few feet of fly line beyond the rod tip, as the leader won't have enough weight to put a bend in a rod. For that matter, don't even practice casting without a leader. The line will not behave as it should without an air-resistant leader on the end to slow it down. You don't need to practice with a fly, though—just a piece of yarn or no fly at all will do fine. Plus, it's much safer.

Do whatever you can to get 15 to 20 feet of line outside of the rod tip. Thrash the rod around and strip line off the reel. Peek ahead in this guide and see how to do a roll cast (see page 77) to get the line out. Or just lay the rod on the ground and manually pull the line out. When you become more proficient, you'll be able to make brisk little false casts while pulling line off the reel, but right now any method that works is just fine.

I have often noticed that beginners either start with too much line or too little. As a general rule, start with two rod-lengths of line. The average trout rod is 8½ feet long. Two rod-lengths will give you almost 20 feet of line, which is perfect to begin with. Don't start with less than 15 feet of line, because things just can't get rolling without some line heavy enough to bend the rod tip. Also, don't start with more line than you can handle smoothly—this will most likely lead to some bad habits. Besides, most fish on the river are caught within 30 feet or less.

THE PICKUP

Get your grip and stance settled and comfortable. Lock the line against the grip with the index (trigger) finger of your casting hand. Start with the rod tip very low, so that it is almost in the water. Raise the rod slowly so that the line begins to slide on the water. Accelerate smoothly but aggressively through the pickup. Don't rip the line off the water. Slide it off gracefully (see illustration on page 26).

Pickup Tips

The pickup is executed primarily with the forearm. Start with the thumb on top of the grip and have the rod angled so the tip is very close to the water. Cock your wrist forward so that the thumb points down the rod shaft and the butt of the rod is parallel with your forearm. Raise the rod by lifting exclusively with your forearm, so that the line begins to slide on the water. Your casting hand should rise up to neck and shoulder level as you lift the rod with your forearm (see page 27).

THE BACKCAST

As the rod nears the vertical position, accelerate and then make an abrupt stop at a point just slightly beyond the vertical. Stop the rod forcibly as the end of the fly line lifts off the water (see page 28). As the rod approaches the vertical position, the wrist should make

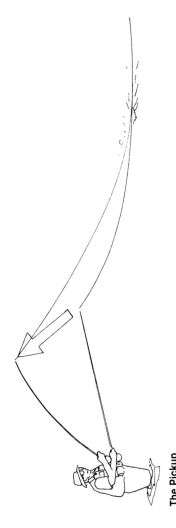

The Pickup
Don't rip the line off of the water! Slide it off gracefully.

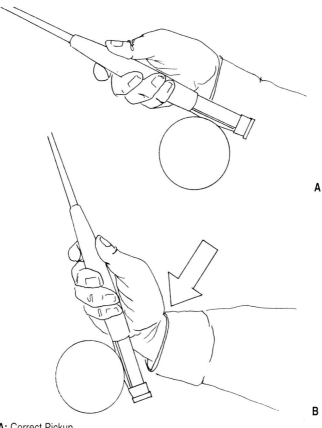

A: Correct Pickup.
Lift the rod with the forearm during the pickup.
B: Incorrect Pickup.
Do not break the wrist during the pickup.

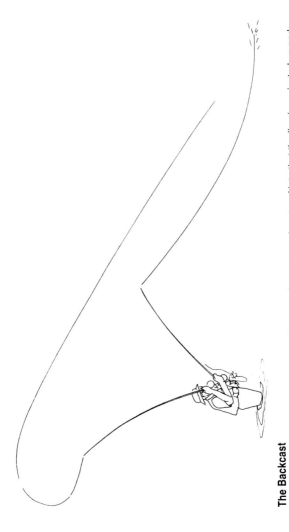

The Backcast
As the rod approaches the vertical position, accelerate to a crisp stop. Note that the line is projected up and behind the caster.

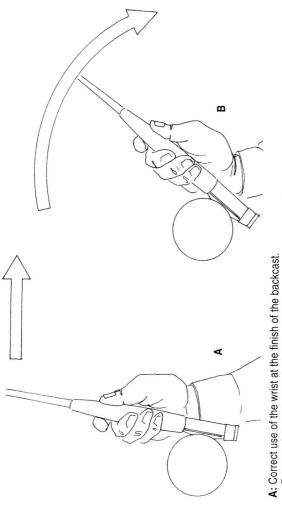

A: Correct use of the wrist at the finish of the backcast.
Proper wrist rotation on the backcast will lead to correct rod position.
B: Do not break the wrist at the finish of the backcast.
Breaking the wrist on the backcast is bad form and will lead to severe casting problems.

a decisive snap. This "wrist snap" should be crisp but not overblown. Correct wrist rotation will project the rod tip upward and slightly behind the caster. Excessive wrist rotation will plunge the tip way past the vertical position, causing a rounded-off "igloo cast" behind you (see page 29). Remember, don't paint the ceiling of an igloo. Try to imagine painting a line across a conventional ceiling at the end of the backcast. The paintbrush should draw a straight line across the ceiling and then flick paint off the brush at the end of the backcast. The wrist snap should *not* force the tip of the rod off of the conventional ceiling.

The wrist snap should pass the tip slightly over the butt of the rod. Once the tip passes over the butt of the rod, the casting loop is formed. Stopping crisply will help form narrow, well-defined loops.

Backcast Tips

Imagine the backcast as really an *up cast:* Try to propel the line upward more than backward. If you were to embed a marshmallow on the tip of the rod, you would flip the marshmallow off only at the end of the stroke, and stop *right after* it pops off the rod tip. The line will travel in whatever direction the marshmallow is tossed. Tossing the imaginary marshmallow up and over your shoulder will elevate the line in an upward direction, allowing the front cast to unfurl downhill. It is, of course, much easier to cast a line downhill rather than uphill.

After a brief pause or stop on the backcast, the line will be fully extended behind you. Now it's time to start the front stroke. Don't wait too long. Allowing the line to fall below the rod tip will create problems for the front cast. The line should be parallel to the ground as you start the front cast. If the line is up and behind you, how do you know when to begin the front cast? Great question! Use an open stance and simply turn your head to see the backcast develop. This will help you to see when the line is completely stretched out and, more important, it will allow you to see where the rod has stopped. The problem I see most often with beginners in our fishing schools is that they don't have any idea where they are stopping the rod at the completion of the backcast. Poor rod position can be cured by just turning your head and watching the development of the backcast.

THE FRONT CAST

The mechanics of the front cast are easy to execute, especially if the line has been correctly positioned with the backcast. The rod has come to a crisp stop, allowing the line to extend fully. Start the forward action slowly. The rod butt will lead the way, moving forward and at a slight angle downward. The rod should begin to bend so that the tip lags well behind the grip and hand. As the rod flexes, smoothly accelerate your cast and project the tip so that it stops abruptly at or about eye level.

Legendary fishing guide Joe Bressler completing a forward cast on Idaho's South Fork of the Snake. Note the flex of the rod, the position of his hand, and the rod tip at eye level.

The wrist plays a major role in the formation of the front cast. As you near the completion of the forward stroke, think of pushing the thumb into the cork grip and pulling back on the pinkie with a decisive wrist snap. Your elbow should remain close to the body as the rod tip is pushed out in front of you. Don't "throw" the rod as you would a baseball. Rather, project the tip out in front of you, stopping it at eye level. The rod tip will come to a halt and the line should unfurl uniformly over the water, landing softly.

Front Cast Tips

Try to think of the front cast as pulling the line forward. Why? While it's nearly impossible to push limp fly line so that it straightens out, it can be easily pulled forward.

Your elbow should remain close to your body, yet not be pressed into it. Years ago fly casting was taught by practicing with a book tucked under the casting arm. The cast was supposed to be executed while the casting elbow held a book in place. This method is too restrictive, however. Although this technique may have been helpful with old soft bamboo rods, it does not apply to today's modern graphite rods. The arm position should feel more like having a grapefruit tucked up in your armpit. The casting arm

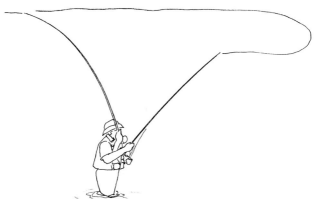

The Front Cast
1: Try to think of the front cast as pulling the line forward. Why? Although it is nearly impossible to push limp fly line so that it straightens out, it can be easily pulled forward.
2: Stop the rod tip abruptly at the finish of the forward stroke and the line will unfurl over the water.

and elbow have much more freedom to move if you are holding up a grapefruit instead of a book. However, if your hand lunges too far forward on the front cast, the grapefruit will fall out. Your casting hand may reach out in front of you, but your elbow should remain close to the body (see illustration on page 33).

After you have completed the forward stroke, lower the rod down to the water to begin another pickup. Repeat this process until loop size and line control are well within your grasp.

RECAP (TIPS TO THINK ABOUT FOR THE PICK UP-AND-LAY DOWN CAST)

- **Tip #1:** Start the rod tip near the surface of the water to begin the pickup portion of your cast. This will cause the rod to load quickly, allowing for an early completion of the backcast.
- **Tip #2:** Open your stance and turn your head to see where the rod is stopping on the backcast.
- **Tip #3:** Try to think of the backcast as an up cast. The line will straighten out with less effort if it is cast upward on the backcast, then down slightly on the front cast. Put another way, it is easier to cast the line up a hill first, then pull it down off a hill on the front stroke.
- **Tip #4:** Do not overrotate your wrist. Use the correct amount of forearm motion, then apply the wrist properly.

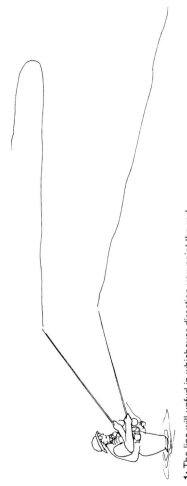

1: The line will unfurl in whichever direction you point the rod.
2: After you have completed the forward stroke, lower the rod to begin another pickup.

- **Tip #5:** Keep your elbow comfortably near your side while you execute the forward cast. Try to project the rod tip forward without throwing your hand with it. Then stop the rod abruptly, at about eye level.

Some other general points that you should keep in mind while casting: First, to make casting nearly effortless, the rod must bend. Fly casting requires very little strength if the rod bends properly. You can cast a fly line with a broomstick, but it's hard work and not very pretty. When you are having a combination of problems, you can often smooth out many of them by focusing on making the rod bend, without worrying unduly about where your wrist and forearm and elbow are pointing.

Second, it is the rod tip that casts the line, not the handle. If you can get your mind off holding the rod and out to where the action is, you will be able to follow directions better and will understand what the rod is doing. Thinking "out near the tip" also helps keep a bend in the rod.

Third, never let the line drop below the rod tip on an overhead cast. This has practical applications, both for casting form and for safety. Any time the line falls below the tip on the backcast, you are robbing your cast of energy that has built up in the spring of the rod. In order to build up maximum energy, the line must be parallel to the ground and pulling the rod tip into a bend. On the forward cast, always keeping the line above the tip of the rod forces you to point the tip in front of you quickly, and prevents tailing loops. And if you always keep the line and leader above the rod tip, you'll never hit yourself with a fly.

Finally, try to maintain tension on the line with the rod tip. Jerky starts and stops that form slack between the rod tip and line introduce sloppiness. Maintaining constant tension with the line gives you the maximum energy from your casts and makes them smoother. It is the constant tension idea that introduces subtle drift or follow-through on a cast, and is a major distinction between a smooth caster and a mediocre thrasher.

CHAPTER 5

THE FOREARM AND WRIST IN FLY CASTING

Finding the correct balance between forearm and wrist motion during the casting stroke is the key to success. Unfortunately, many antiquated theories state that the wrist should be locked in place or its motion should be completely minimized during the casting stroke. This is absolutely false! It is the motion of the wrist that forms casting loops. If you lock out the wrist, the line will run into itself and cause what is known as a tailing loop. Excessive wrist rotation applied at the wrong time will lead to casting problems. You can bend the wrist; just don't break it.

What does "breaking the wrist" mean? Place your casting arm loosely at your side and point your rod straight out over the water, parallel to the surface. Notice the angle between your wrist and forearm. This is the position to maintain throughout the cast, with just a few degrees variation when introducing the wrist snap on the power stroke. You should start your cast in this position and end in this position. If not, you're doing something wrong and will need to analyze your form.

The amount of wrist movement should be controlled and applied with proper timing in the casting stroke. On the backcast, just a small break of the wrist can dump the tip of the rod behind you, because a slight variation in motion at the grip is magnified over the length of the rod into a difference of several feet. Just remember that it is the rod tip, and not the handle, that casts the line. This alone will keep you from breaking your wrist. On the forward cast, breaking the wrist will drive the rod tip toward the surface of the water instead of out over the water. This makes the line slam into the water and land in a pile, not to mention forming a tailing loop. Bad stuff.

TROUBLESHOOTING

1. **Problem:** The line is piling up and not completely straightening out at the completion of the cast. This is by far the most common problem that beginners encounter, and there are countless reasons why this will happen. Following is a short list of a few of the most common reasons why the line will not effectively turn over:

   • **Cause #1:** If you cast as if you are painting the ceiling of an igloo, your line will look like a pile of linguini at the end of the cast. Incorrect casting form in this instance is a result of the rod tip traveling in a rounded-off fashion, leading to excessively open casting loops that cannot adequately turn over the fly line.

   • **Solution:** Adjust the size of your casting arc to match the amount of line you are casting. Also, try to draw the rod tip in a straighter, more direct path between the stopping points of your cast. Most new fly casters have a casting arc that is too wide for the amount of line they are trying to handle. Imagine painting a conventional ceiling on the backcast. This will keep you from rounding off your casting stroke excessively.

- **Cause #2:** The backcast is underpowered in relation to the front cast.
- **Solution:** Don't lag the line out of the water and then try to force a long front cast aggressively. The backcast and front cast should be mirror images of each other. The tempo of the backcast should be just as crisp as the tempo of the front cast. Most new casters I teach have trouble understanding that the form and energy of the backcast dictates how well the front cast is formed.
- **Cause #3:** Waving the rod rather than casting it.
- **Solution:** Don't aimlessly wave the rod through the casting arc. Make a definitive finish at the completion of the back and front casts. Form narrow casting loops by stopping the rod decisively after the tip passes over the rod butt.

2. **Problem:** The line is slapping on the water.
   - **Cause:** Driving the line into the water is caused by dropping the rod too low on the forward cast.
   - **Solution:** Don't let the rod tip point below horizontal. Try to stop the rod near eye level, so that the line will extend cleanly over the water. The casting arc may also be tilted forward ex-

cessively. If so, adjust the angle so your finish is down and out rather than just down.

3. **Problem:** Your casting arm tires quickly when casting.

   • **Cause:** You are doing what I call "Statue of Liberty Cast"—your hand is raised too high during the casting stroke.

   • **Solution:** Lower your casting hand during the casting stroke. Your elbow should remain below shoulder level. When you are making casts of less than 40 feet, your casting hand should not rise above your head.

PART TWO

REFINING YOUR CASTING STROKE

GOAL: To refine your casting style by controlling the flex of the rod throughout the entire stroke, and to develop the ability to shoot line, false cast, and roll cast.

CHAPTER 6

APPLYING POWER TO THE CASTING MOTION

How is it that an expert can make fly casting look wonderfully effortless, while others seem to cross fly casting with aerobics in an exhausting attempt to lay out a mere 15 feet of line? With proper timing and by using just enough strength, the expert has learned to harness the bend or flex of the fly rod. This bending action represents stored energy, and skillful casters use that energy to propel the line. In essence they make the rod work for them, rather than aimlessly waving it around in the air.

The application of power has many names in our sport. The terms **power stroke, power snap,** or **speed up and stop** are all used interchangeably. This "power stroke" may be difficult to grasp at first, but it is the key to developing a consistent fly-casting style.

First, you must have a feeling of "loading" the rod. This means that you can actually feel the rod bending or flexing during the casting motion. To correctly load the rod, you must progressively exert more power or force smoothly throughout the casting stroke. What does this mean? It means that force is used sparingly at the start but is applied directly before the rod comes to a halt. Try to gracefully accelerate the rod tip to an abrupt stop. Think of the motion as throwing a dart. You wouldn't just whip the dart at the bull's-eye. You would start easy, then apply a decisive wrist snap at the end. Keep in mind that power needs to be applied equally on the backcast as well as on the front cast. Do not exert more force on one part or the other.

One of my favorite ways to illustrate this is with the "marshmallow tip," which I referred to earlier. Imagine embedding a marshmallow on to the tip of your rod. Begin both the back and front casts smoothly, gradually bending the rod so that the marshmallow stays on throughout the stroke. If you force a bend in the rod too quickly, the marshmallow will fall off prematurely. At

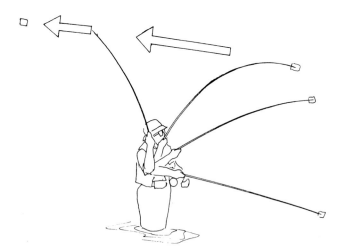

A: Power Stroke: "Marshmallow Tip on the Backcast"
Power is applied correctly if you can smoothly hold the marshmallow on the tip of the rod until it is ejected at the finish of the backcast.

the completion of both forward and backcasts, try to eject the marshmallow off your rod at eye level, by driving the rod tip to an abrupt stop. Remember that the line will travel in whatever direction you flip off the marshmallow, or whatever direction the rod tip stops.

MORE ON THE FOREARM AND WRIST IN FLY CASTING

The forearm muscles do the majority of the work in fly casting, but it is the wrist that applies the power stroke.

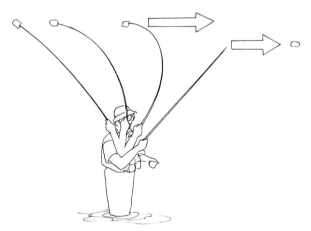

B: Power Stroke: "Marshmallow Tip on the Front Cast"
The same holds true for the power stroke on the forward cast. The marshmallow should be held on the tip of the rod by smoothly applying power throughout the cast. Eject the marshmallow at the end of the stroke by stopping the rod abruptly.

The motion of fly casting is initiated with the forearm. You need to start the backcast and front cast with the forearm, but the finishing move is completed with a decisive, yet controlled, wrist rotation or snap. How much forearm and wrist depends on how much line you are trying to cast—60 feet of line requires a different casting arc than 10 feet of fly line does. Let's examine the mechanics of the forearm and wrist with short, medium, and long casts.

Short Casts

When casting shorter amounts of line—20 feet or less—the casting arc is very small, and you do not need excessive flex in the rod. Short casts require less energy, and just the tip of the rod can provide enough

A small stream is the place to perfect your short, accurate casts.

flex to lay out the line. This can be accomplished with a slight movement of the forearm and a minimal wrist rotation. Think of casting with a firm forearm and wrist, but move the rod tip at the end of the stroke exclusively with the wrist. The movement should be controlled, so the forearm and wrist are solid throughout the movement. The acceleration to the stop is applied

Short Casts

On short casts the forearm and wrist work almost in unison. The wrist rotation is minimal; the distance the casting hand travels is also minimal because of the small casting arc.

at the end of the cast with a crisp wrist snap. Casting problems will arise if you let your wrist break to finish the cast, however. This is true for the backcast as well as the front cast.

Notice that the casting hand travels a short distance when you're throwing a short line. Due to the length of the fly rod when handling less line, it may only take a slight movement of the wrist and forearm to dramatically effect tip movement. In effect, micro-movements of the casting hand lead to macro-movements at the tip (see illustration on page 49).

Medium-Distance Casts

Slightly longer casts require more energy—and to produce more energy, you must increase the flex of the rod tip. Rather than trying to cram all that energy into a narrow casting arc, you will widen it to provide for a smoother casting motion. And by widening the arc, you can progressively increase the flex in the rod, which in turn will provide greater energy. This will allow for a longer cast to be made.

The mechanics of the forearm and wrist will adapt to cast through a longer arc: The casting hand will have to travel slightly farther due to the increased bending action and expanded casting arc. When adapting to a longer casting stroke, the forearm and wrist will remain stiff at the onset and the casting hand will travel through a longer arc. Then, at the end of the stroke, the wrist rotation will be applied. It is still forearm first, then wrist: It's just that the forearm and wrist

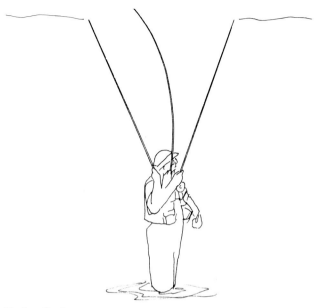

Medium Cast
On medium-distance casts the casting hand will have to travel farther due to the expended casting arc. Note that the wrist bends more than on shorter casts, but does not break.

will move as a unit throughout a longer motion before the wrist snap is applied in a crisp finishing move. It should be more like *foooorrrrreearm,* then *wrist.*

Long Casts

When casting very long lines, it is imperative to harness the full potential of the fly rod. The butt section, or bottom part, of the rod is the most stiff and stores the most energy. The only way to increase the flex of the fly rod is to have the casting hand travel a greater distance through a larger casting arc. The mechanics of the forearm and wrist thus become further separated. The wrist position remains intact as the forearm drives the casting hand through an increased arc. Once again the wrist will bend, but not break, as it accelerates to a clean snap at the completion of the stroke. Note that the casting hand moves through a longer stroke than it does when casting a shorter line, and that the elbow is raised to shoulder height (see illustration). Remember that the size of the casting arc is determined by how much line is being cast.

Tailing Loops

If you hit your rod with the line or leader while casting, you are throwing a "tailing loop." If you hook your fly on the leader, you're throwing a tailing loop. And if you find odd overhand knots (wind knots) in your leader, you guessed it—tailing loops again. Tailing loops occur when the fly line runs into itself or the casting loop implodes. Most tailing loops are caused by overpowering the rod and shocking the tip prematurely through the casting motion. To avoid this, your casting motion must be smooth and the acceleration must culminate in a decisive finishing move. In other words, the fly-casting stroke is a smooth speed-up to an abrupt stop.

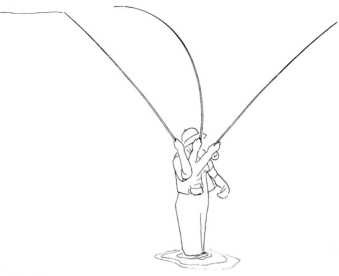

Long Casts

On long casts the casting hand travels even farther, to accommodate for the expanded casting arc. The forearm and wrist rotation become more separated on longer casts. Wrist rotation may increase on long casts, but the wrist still does not break.

Think of hammering a nail into the wall. You wouldn't just haul off and try to whack the nail home immediately. Rather, you would move the hammer quietly at the start, then apply some power right before the head hits the nail. However, once you hit the nail on the head, the motion would stop abruptly. (Try to think of casting a fly rod as using a two-headed hammer: Hit the nail on the backcast as well as the front cast.) If you try to force the rod prematurely, the flex or bend cannot be sustained throughout the entire casting arc. As a result the rod flex will "unload" too soon and a well-defined casting loop can't be formed.

If the tip passes over the handle of the rod in the middle of the stroke rather than at the end of it, a tailing loop will be formed. Correct fly-casting loops are formed at the *end* of the stroke. For smoother casts, maintain the bend in the rod for the entire stroke, so that the tip lags behind throughout the motion and is forced over the butt of the rod at the completion of the cast (see illustration on page 53).

Another cause of tailing loops is a rod tip that travels in a concave path. This is the opposite of the "igloo cast," in which the path of the rod traces a convex shape. Avoid either extreme. Try to draw the rod tip in a straight, more direct line.

Stopping the rod too high at the finish of the front stroke also causes tailing loops. On the forward stroke, avoid pushing the casting hand and thumb only forward. Try to pull your pinkie toward you as you push your thumb down and out. This grip will feel like holding a hammer and hitting a nail down and out. This will clear the tip out of the way as the fly line travels forward. Although I have told you there is little follow-through on a fly cast, you must have some. Complete your forward cast, then lower the rod tip smoothly and without power to waist level, parallel to the water. A big, open loop is better than one that col-

Tailing Loop
A tailing loop like this is formed because the flex in the rod is released or unloaded prematurely in the casting stroke. This is caused by harshly shocking the rod through the cast.

lapses on itself; at least you won't slam the rod with your fly (see illustration on page 57).

The casting arc may also be too small for the amount of line you are trying to cast. If the arc is too small, you will have to whip through the movement. Many times this is mistaken for overpowering the rod. It's really not. It's just that the rod cannot generate enough bend to propel the line in such a confined area.

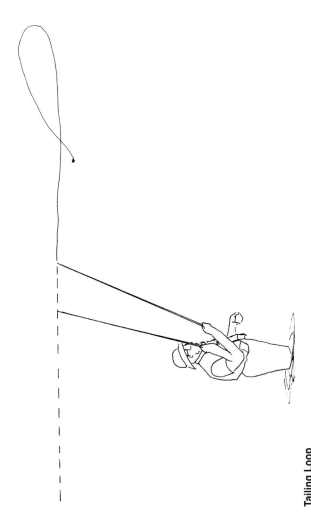

Tailing Loop
This tailing loop is caused because the rod tip stopped too soon—directly in the path of the fly line.

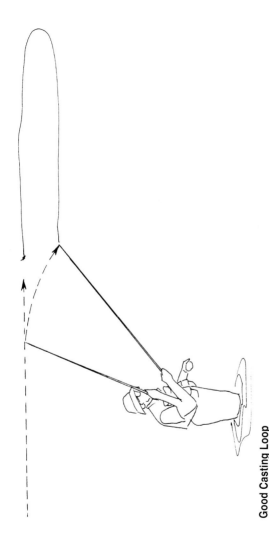

Good Casting Loop
A proper casting loop is formed when the rod tip is stopped cleanly, below the path of the fly line.

57

To compensate, the caster sometimes tries to force the action. If the arc were widened or if perhaps the amount of line were shortened, this problem would be solved. The solution, in other words, is to adjust the casting arc so that it conforms to the amount of line that is being cast.

CHAPTER 7

THE LINE HAND AND SHOOTING LINE

THE LINE HAND

After the pick up-and-lay down cast, the next step in the Orvis Progressive Casting Method is the introduction of the line hand. To learn how to master the fundamentals, practice the casting motion by pinching the line against the grip with the first two fingers of your casting hand. Once you can control the basic motion, free the line from the cork grip and control the line with your left (opposite) hand. Fly fishing is a two-handed sport: The line hand is critical, because it helps you develop line control and reduce slack while fishing.

Start by pulling off two arm lengths of extra line from the reel and let it hang freely. Hold the rod in your right (casting) hand and pinch the line between the thumb and forefinger of your left (noncasting) hand. Tend the fly line so there is no slack between the stripping guide and the line hand. The rest of the excess slack should form a long U-shape that will dangle near your knees (see page 60).

The next step is simple: Just execute the basic pick up-and-lay down cast while holding the line near your belt buckle with the line hand. Change nothing in your casting motion. Maintain some tension on the line between your left hand and the stripping guide. If slack appears, there is a flaw in your casting stroke. Most

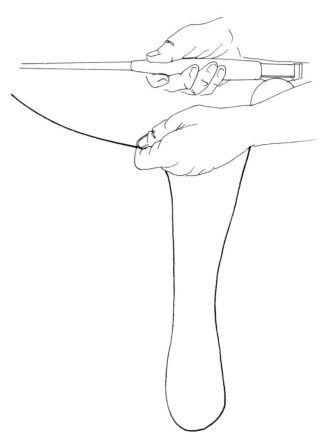

Line Hand
Once you have mastered the basic cast, release the line from your casting hand and hold it in your line hand.

THE ORVIS STREAMSIDE GUIDE TO FLY CASTING

likely the stopping points of your casting arc are incorrect, or the timing of your power stroke is off.

Don't let the line slip through your fingers as the rod is traveling between the forward and backcasts. If you let the line slip prematurely while the rod is in motion, the flex cannot be maintained and the pick up-and-lay down cast will falter.

Although you are freeing the line from the grip, the line will still be under some tension as you hold it with your left (noncasting) hand. This will produce additional flex in the rod, which in turn will increase your line speed. Practice the basic stroke in this fashion until the line can be laid out with sufficient line speed and control.

SHOOTING LINE

Once you have sufficient line speed and loop control, it is time to start shooting line at the finish of the pick up-and-lay down cast. Although it is a serviceable cast, the pick up-and-lay down cast does have its limitations. Many fishing situations will call for adding line to increase the distance of your presentation. Shooting line at this stage of the progression is done on the forward cast only.

If you want to shoot line correctly on the front cast, *concentrate on the backcast.* Many of my students initially try to shoot line by concentrating exclusively on the forward stroke. They subsequently let their backcast fall apart. Remember, if the backcast is poor, the

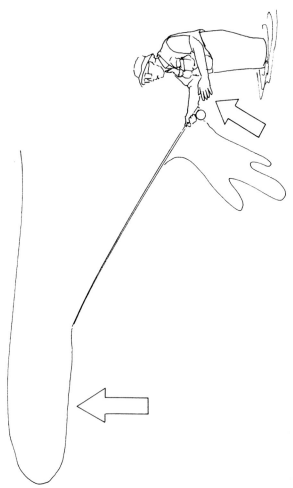

Shooting Line
After the rod comes to a stop and a casting loop is formed, let go of the line with your line hand and it will sail through the guides. Timing is the key; don't let go too soon or hold on too long.

front cast will be poor. If the backcast lacks sufficient line speed or proper loop control, then shooting line becomes difficult.

Begin by feeding 20 to 25 feet of line out beyond the rod tip. Have about 10 feet of extra line in reserve, enough so that it hangs near your feet or a little touches the ground. The slack line at your feet is the amount you will shoot at the finish of the forward stroke. Before you start, make sure there is no slack between your line hand and the first guide on the rod.

Shooting line is actually quite simple. The fundamentals of the pick up-and-lay down cast remain unchanged. However, at the completion of the forward stroke, you release line and let it sail through the guides. The casting hand dictates the stroke, but it's the timing of letting go with the line hand that determines how the well the line will shoot through the guides on the rod. If you let go of the line too soon during the forward motion, the flex in the rod will unload prematurely and the cast will lose energy. Conversely, if you hold the line too long at the finish, you will choke off the momentum of the line.

Timing is critical. You must let go of the line at the completion of the power stroke, at about the same time the rod comes to a stop. After the power is applied, quickly release the line as the rod tip comes to a halt. It helps to think of the order as *stop and let go,* not let go, then stop. This all happens so quickly that it will feel like you are releasing the line at the same time you stop the rod.

Note that you cannot let go of the line until the casting loop is formed. For shorter casts, loops are formed very quickly and the line is released just as the rod comes to a stop. On longer casts, the loops take longer to develop. Subsequently the line is held just a bit longer, allowing for the casting loop to form. Once you see the end of the fly line pass by your head on the front cast, let go with your line hand (see illustration on page 62). Practice shooting line until you can make it fly at will. It is really fun to see line successfully shoot out over the water. Let it fly!

Controlling and Retrieving Line

As you develop the ability to shoot line, learn to control it. Release the line by forming a circle with the thumb and index finger of your left hand and allow the line to run through it as shoots through the rod tip. Your line hand will form an "OK" sign, as if to say it is "OK" to let the line go. This will allow you to control the line as it is presented, and sets you up for an effective retrieve (see illustration on page 65).

Once the line has shot through the rod tip and has landed on the water, you will need to retrieve it so you can cast again. In fly fishing you manipulate the fly by retrieving with your line hand, not with the reel, as in spin fishing. You can accurately control the speed and action of your flies by stripping in the line with your left (noncasting) hand.

Start with the rod tip low, near the water. Grab the line with your left hand and hang it over the forefinger or middle finger (or both) of your casting hand while holding the rod. Retrieve the line by pulling it in strips from *behind* your finger. Do not reach in front of the casting hand and replace the line in the middle finger for each strip (see illustration on page 66).

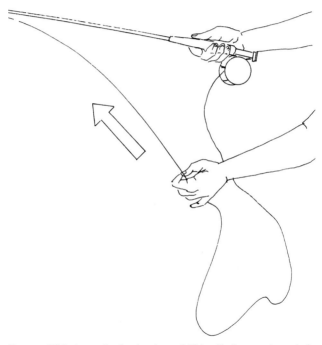

Form on "OK" sign as the line is released. This will allow you to control the line as it is presented, which will set you up for an effective retrieve.

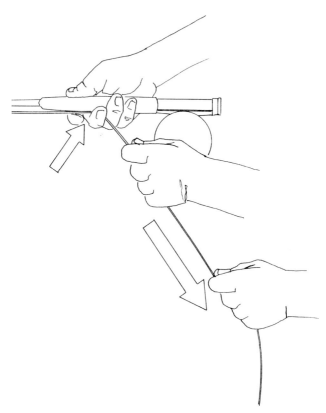

Retrieving Line
Hook the line behind the middle or forefinger of your rod hand and retrieve by pulling from behind that finger.

CHAPTER 8

FALSE CASTING

J ust as the name suggests, a false cast is not actually a presentation cast, but rather a way of holding line aloft in a series of casts where the line never touches the water. This technique is used for measuring distance or for changing the direction of the cast. A false cast is also used to dry off a floating fly that has become waterlogged.

At the completion of the front stroke, don't let the line drop to the water as it unfolds. Just stop the rod tip at the finish of the front stroke without any follow-through, wait for it to straighten above the water, and make a backcast. Stopping the rod tip a bit higher on the forward arc will let the line unfurl above the water rather than on it. Try to develop a rhythm. At first make only one false cast, then lay the line back down on the water. Once you have control of one, try two false casts and then present the line. I do not recommend doing more than four false casts, as even a slight error in timing is tough to correct while false casting. The longer your fly is in the air, the greater the chance you'll run into trouble.

A false cast requires a strong sense of timing. Remember that both the front and backcasts take equal time to unfold. To help develop your timing, it's helpful to open your stance and watch the backcast unroll (see illustrations).

1: A normal pickup and backcast are made.

2: On the backcast, the line must extend fully behind the caster. Then a forward false cast is begun.

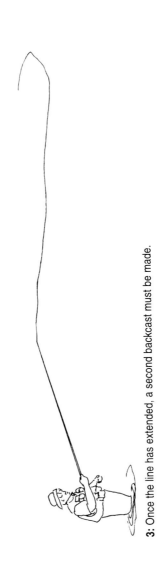

3: Once the line has extended, a second backcast must be made.

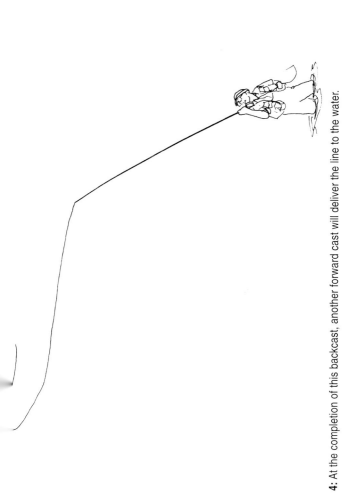

4: At the completion of this backcast, another forward cast will deliver the line to the water.

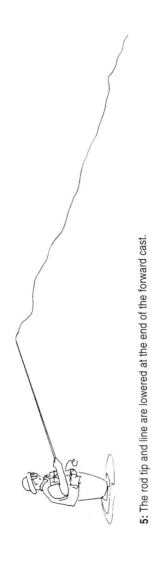

5: The rod tip and line are lowered at the end of the forward cast.

It's beautiful to see the line gracefully dance back and forth, but don't become hypnotized by it. False casting is great for practicing, but you can't catch a fish unless the fly is on the water. The only thing a false cast will catch is a tree branch. So practice false casting to develop casting rhythm and timing, but don't overdo it.

CHANGING CASTING PLANES

When fly casting, the rod path should stay in a vertical plane and the line should remain parallel to the ground. This means the path of the rod should travel in a straight line as it moves back and forth. This harnesses casting energy efficiently and gives you more power and control.

The casting plane or path that the rod takes should change depending on the fishing situation. For example, you may need to cast almost side-arm to place a fly under an overhanging tree. Sometimes it's also helpful to lower the angle or casting plane to get under gusts of wind.

As long as the line remains parallel to the ground, you can cast directly overhead or completely side-arm. Most beginners trying to learn the stroke find it easier to cast in a more up and down fashion, with a casting plane that is directly overhead. This overhead style allows the caster to use his or her head as a reference for stopping points in the cast. The casting hand on the back stroke will come up and stop next to the eye or ear. It is a way to associate rod positions with a fixed point rather than just aimlessly waving the rod to an imaginary spot in the air. Legendary caster Joan Wulff takes this one step further; she sometimes teaches new students to lift the rod directly at their forehead on the backcast. No one in their right mind would allow the rod to go back too far, because it would hit them right between the eyes. That is really using the head as a reference point!

As they develop a feel for the cast, most fly rodders will choose an arc that falls somewhere between directly overhead and completely side-arm casting. Think of it. If you tried throwing a football, you would not whip it directly overhead and whiz it right by your ear. You also would not try to throw it with your hand at belt level. Holding the forearm and elbow at about a 45-degree angle creates a comfortable casting plane that is slightly side-arm (see illustration).

The casting arc and rod path should remain intact as the plane is angled more toward side-arm. Imagine that the rod tip has a paintbrush on it. Instead of painting the ceiling directly overhead, imagine dropping the casting angle slightly, to a side-arm motion. Now imagine painting a line on the point where the wall meets the ceiling. For a complete side cast, imagine painting a line on the wall at waist level. Remember, paint a flat wall—don't paint the side wall of an igloo. If the rod tip travels in a rounded-off, semicircular path, your line will form excessively open casting loops and your stroke will falter. Even when you drop the casting arc on its side, the size of the arc remains the same and the rod tip should follow a straight line.

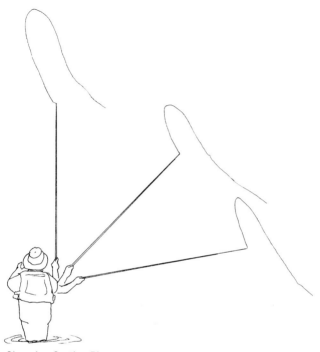

Changing Casting Planes
Fly casting is not performed exclusively overhead. Change casting planes as your skills improve and fishing conditions dictate.

FALSE CASTING, THEN SHOOTING LINE

Once you have developed the skills of false casting and shooting line separately, it's time to combine the two. Being able to false cast and hold your line aloft and then shoot it is an invaluable skill to have. You must be able to effectively control line as you false cast, then shoot it on the forward stroke before you can effectively fish upstream with nymphs or dry flies. The false cast is ideal for measuring the amount of line you are handling, and shooting line will permit you reach your target effectively.

When combining these two skills, make a single false cast, then shoot some line on your delivery. Once you can handle one, make two false casts, and so on. But don't attempt more than four false casts, as excessive false casting can spook fish. False casting may look pretty, but it can also wear you out, so keep it to a minimum.

CHAPTER 9

ROLL CASTING

The roll cast is used to present the fly in situations where there is little or no room for a backcast. In fact, the roll cast does not require a backcast at all. As its name implies, the roll cast is executed by unfurling or rolling the line over the water with a simple forward cast. Say you are fishing the edge of a deep, tree-lined lake and can't wade out more than 10 feet, but you need to reach fish that are a good 30 feet out from shore. Although a roll cast offers neither the accuracy, delivery, nor distance of the overhead cast, it will get your line out to the fish.

A requirement of the roll cast is that the end of the line be under tension as the cast is being made. Some of the fly line must remain on the water as the stroke is executed. It is best to practice this cast on a pond or some type of still water. If you try to roll cast on grass, the surface tension will not enable you to roll out the fly line.

Start with 20 to 25 feet of line extended beyond the tip of the rod. Pinch the line against the cork grip with one or two fingers of your casting hand. (It is best to learn this cast with just one hand at first.) Raise the rod slowly and slide the line on the water smoothly back toward you. There is no acceleration at the beginning of the roll cast, so don't overdo it and jerk the line out of the water. Bring the line back to you with the rod

Tom Rosenbauer helping his daughter Brooke with a roll cast in a tight spot. Note the loop of line behind the rod.

tilted to the side, about 10 degrees from the vertical. This will keep the line off to one side, so it does not slam into the rod when you make the cast.

Raise your casting hand higher than you would for a normal cast. Bring the fly reel up to about ear level as you draw it back, and cock your wrist more than you would for an overhead cast, so that the tip is well behind you. Try to break your wrist more on this cast. This will cause the tip to extend farther back, which will put some line behind you and your rod hand. (You can't make this cast without some line behind you.) The longer the roll cast, the more line you will need behind you. The line will form a large semicircle that extends from the tip of the rod to the water at your feet.

A

B

The Roll Cast
1A: To properly make a roll cast, make sure some line is behind you and that the end of the line is anchored in the water. Start the cast by pulling down on the rod with the forearm.
1B: The rod should be tilted to the side slightly, so that the cast can unfurl to the inside of the line on the water.

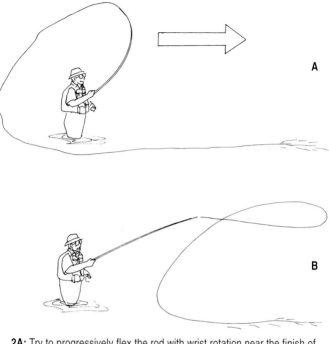

2A: Try to progressively flex the rod with wrist rotation near the finish of the stroke.
2B: As the rod unloads, stop the tip abruptly near eye level.

The rest of the line should remain on the water in front of you. Make sure that the line comes to a complete stop before you try to roll it forward.

Start the roll cast with a break in your wrist, so that the rod is tilted back at an angle that is around 2:30 on that same clock reference. Begin the roll cast by

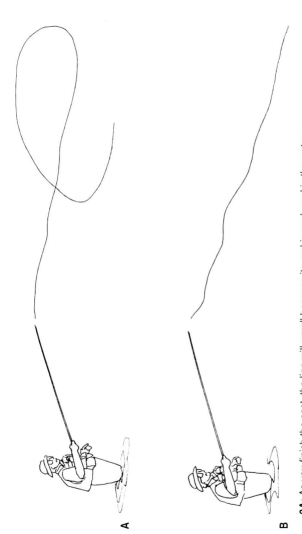

3A: As you finish the cast, the line will unroll because its end is anchored in the water.
3B: After the cast is made, lower the rod to begin another roll cast.

A

B

81

pulling down with the forearm so that the tip lags behind as the rod starts to bend. As you finish the cast, drive the tip forward by rotating your wrist and pushing on your thumb. Try to bend the rod in a smooth motion as you drive it forward. It should have a slow start with an acceleration to a complete stop, just like a normal forward cast. In fact, it's virtually the same forward motion (see page 81).

End with the rod tip near eye level so that the line rolls out over the water. Don't push the rod tip down too low or the line will pile up on the water. Remember, the fly line will unroll in whichever direction the rod tip stops (see page 80). Point it to the eye and see it fly!

TROUBLESHOOTING

1. **Problem:** After you start using the line hand, the cast will not completely straighten out.
   • **Cause:** The line hand is not providing tension as the cast is executed. As a result, line is being leaked into the casting motion and the bend in the rod is being prematurely unloaded.
   • **Solution:** Secure the line with the thumb and forefinger of the left hand and hold the line under tension for the duration of the casting motion. Make sure you don't change the shape or the size of the casting arc just because the line hand has been introduced. You should still be casting the same amount of line as when the line was locked against the grip.

2. **Problem:** The line will not effectively shoot through the rod at the completion of front cast.
   - **Cause #1:** You're releasing the line with improper timing. Holding on for too long after the cast has been made will choke off the line's momentum. Conversely, letting go of the line too early during the forward stroke will cause the bend in the rod to "unload" prematurely, and there will be no energy left to shoot the line.
   - **Solution #1:** Let go of the line only at the finish of the forward cast. Try to release the line as the rod comes to a stop. Once you can see the end of the line pass overhead on the forward stroke, release the line and it should sail out through the guides. Don't let go and then cast—rather, cast, then let go.
   - **Cause #2:** The actual casting stroke may be below par, with a lack of line speed and loop control.
   - **Solution #2:** Correctly shooting line requires narrow, well-defined casting loops. Develop proper shape to your casting loops before trying to shoot line.
3. **Problem:** The end of the line is hitting the water while you're false casting.
   - **Cause:** The stopping point of the rod tip is too low on the front cast. The size of the casting arc may also be too large for the amount of line being cast. This will lead to uncontrollable

casting loops as you false cast, which will cause the line to slap on the water.

- **Solution:** When presenting the line on the water, the rod tip should stop at or just below eye level. When attempting to false cast, stop the rod tip higher than eye level. This will allow the line to unfurl higher over the surface of the water.

  Try false casting with 15 feet of line beyond the rod tip when you practice. It is very easy to control and false cast shorter amounts of line. Then, as you progress, add some line and expand the casting arc.

  The amount of line you can handle when false casting varies with the size of the rod, the type of line, and your own casting ability. As a rule-of-thumb, never try to false cast more than 35 feet with a trout rod or 50 feet with a saltwater rod.

4. **Problem:** Tailing loops—the fly is hitting the rod tip or the line as it is being cast.
   - **Cause:** You are overpowering and "shocking" the rod through the casting motion. The bend or flex in the rod is harshly exerted and is not being controlled throughout the cast.
   - **Solution:** Smooth out your casting. Try not to jerk when starting the casting motion. Begin the stroke smoothly and apply power progressively throughout the casting stroke. Apply the power just before the rod comes to a halt. Each cast is a gradual speed-up to an abrupt stop. Tip: Open up your casting loops and develop

the control to adjust loop size at will. Slightly open loops are going to be better than tailing ones.

5. **Problem:** When roll casting, the line does not completely unfurl and the line piles up at the end of the cast.

- **Cause:** The casting hand is not raised high enough and there is not enough line behind the rod to start the roll cast.

- **Solution:** Raise your casting hand high (near head level) as you draw the line in. Holding your hand high will allow you to generate more momentum and rod bend as the roll cast is executed. Next, break your wrist slightly. This will push the tip farther back and put some line behind you and the rod. The more line behind you and the rod, the easier the roll cast will be. If some line is not behind the rod at the start of the roll cast, the line will not unfurl.

PART THREE

ADVANCED FLY CASTING

GOAL: To effectively control and cast longer distances of line in a variety of fishing conditions with the use of the double haul.

CHAPTER 10

THE SINGLE HAUL AND DOUBLE HAUL

Once you attempt to cast beyond 40 or 50 feet, the casting hand alone can not produce enough flex in a fly rod to present the line. **Hauling,** or pulling the line with precision as the rod moves through the paces, will produce additional tension as the line is working through the guides. This tension, in turn will cause the rod to flex more, providing increased casting energy.

There are many advantages to mastering the magic of the double haul. Not only will it help you cast longer and farther, but it will also increase your line control and speed—which will improve your casts at any distance. For short casts, hauling can help to straighten out longer leaders and control the slack line between the casting hand and guide surfaces. Learning to haul correctly makes fly casting easier with any length of line, and all accomplished fly casters should master its secrets.

THE SINGLE HAUL

Before jumping right into the intricate timing of the double haul, first learn to make a single haul on the back-cast. This is the initial step in the double haul anyway, so it is a perfect starting point. You can also perform a single haul exclusively on the front cast, but for the purpose of learning, start by hauling only on the back stroke.

Hauling will permit you to pick up and present more line than a conventional cast, so start with 35 to 45 feet of line extended beyond the rod tip. Begin with the rod tip near the surface of the water. Reach up and grab the line within 6 inches of the stripping guide and have 10 to 15 feet of slack in reserve at your feet. Grabbing the line close to the first guide will reduce any chance for slack to form between the line hand and stripping guide at the start of the stroke. Slack is your worst enemy when you are learning to haul.

Next, start the casting motion by slowly raising the rod. Hold the line securely in your left (noncasting) hand throughout the cast. Raise the rod and the line hand together as you begin the cast. Once the rod approaches the vertical position, apply more power with a quick and decisive stroke by raising your casting hand to near head level and shoving the tip of the rod back to about the 2 o'clock position. As you drive the rod through the back stroke, pull on the line with the left hand at the same time. Timing is crucial, so haul with the left (line) hand exactly at the same time you power the rod. Try to maintain some tension with the line hand as you make the haul. Don't overdo it and pull too far as you haul. Instead of a long pull, make the haul a short, crisp tug. When you are learning to haul correctly, your hands should never separate more than two feet.

The haul should stop when the rod comes to a halt. Stop your stroke sharply so the bend in the rod unloads and delivers the line powerfully behind you. The combination of pulling on the line with a well-timed power stroke should allow you to pick up all the line on the water and cast it decisively up and behind you.

Finally, drive the rod forward with your casting hand and stop the tip at eye level. Let go of the line at the finish of the front cast and shoot it out over the water. Hauling correctly on the backcast will actually help improve your front stroke. You will be able to shoot more line effectively just by hauling properly on the backcast. Because a single haul puts more energy and line speed into the backcast, it's often helpful to do this when you have the wind at your back. Tail winds can collapse your backcast. Hauling compensates by helping you slice through the wind. You are handling more line, which makes this a longer cast, so expand the casting arc. This will permit the rod and casting hand to travel through a longer stroke. However, don't overextend: Your elbow should be near your side and bent slightly at the completion of the backcast. Try not to overwork yourself—make the rod flex and lay out the line for you (see illustration on page 92).

Recap: Tips to Think About for the Single Haul

- **Tip #1:** Start with the rod tip low. Hold the line so there is no slack between the first guide and the left hand.
- **Tip #2:** Raise the rod smoothly and begin to accelerate as the rod reaches the vertical position.
- **Tip #3:** Increase the bend of the rod by applying the power stroke, and pull the on the line with the left hand at the same moment.

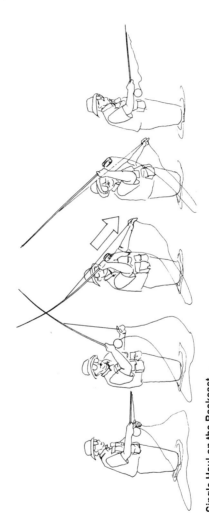

Single Haul on the Backcast
The haul is executed with the line hand at the same time the power is applied with the wrist snap of the casting hand.

92

- **Tip #4:** Stop the rod sharply and allow the line to unfurl behind you.
- **Tip #5:** Make a forward cast and let the line go with your left (noncasting) hand as the rod comes to a stop. The line should fly out of the rod, drawing up the excess slack that was at your feet.

Practice the single haul on the backcast until you have complete control over the tension with your line hand. If you can haul with precise timing and no slack appears between the line hand and the guides, you are ready for the double haul.

THE DOUBLE HAUL

The double haul is really just two single hauls—one applied on the backcast and one on the front cast. The key to unlocking the timing of the double haul is to learn how to effectively reposition the line hand after making the first haul on the back stroke.

Again, start with more line out over the tip. Make a few normal overhead casts until you have 35 to 45 feet of line in front of you. In this case, more line is better than less, so don't try to make it easier by practicing with 30 feet of line; it won't work. The added weight of the extra line helps to reposition the line hand after the first haul is made.

The Back Haul

Complete a single haul on the backcast. Before you attempt the front cast, reposition your left (line) hand so

Guide Frank Catino completing a double haul in
the Florida Keys. His line hand will drift back to
the stripping guide as he shoots the line.

that a haul can be made on the front cast. After pulling
on the line, your hands should be about 24 inches apart.
Don't pull excessively on the back haul—that keeps the
hands too far apart, making it harder to control slack in
the line. It also makes it harder for the line hand to drift
back to the reel for the second haul on the front cast.

At the completion of the backcast haul, the line hand drifts back to meet the reel in a quick bouncing move. The line that was pulled with the line hand on the backcast must be given back, so that a haul can be made on the front stroke. The two hands should end up together, near your head.

Most students have trouble with this drift and repositioning of the line hand back to the reel. Imagine that the line between your left (line) hand and the first guide on the rod is actually a large rubber band. After you have hauled on the backcast, the line hand should bounce back to the reel due to the tension of the rubber cord. The line will not actually pull your hand back up to the reel. It is simply a quick "down-up" motion (see illustration on page 96).

The Front Haul

The two hands are together, back up near head level at the finish of the backcast. Both hands move forward together as the front cast begins. At the start of the front cast, imagine using the line to pull down on the rod, so that the butt is pointing out slightly in front of you. Make the rod bend progressively throughout the stroke. Near the finish of the cast, apply the power stroke with the wrist, by pushing your thumb and pulling the pinkie. The front haul is executed simultaneously by pulling on the line with the left hand. Both hands work in unison: As your right hand applies the power to the rod with a wrist snap, your left hand pulls on the line at the same moment.

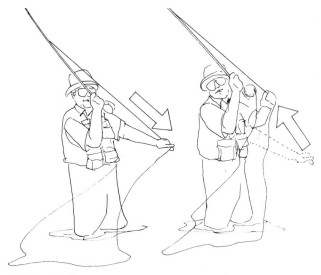

Line Hand Drift

After a haul is made on the backcast, the line hand will drift back to the casting hand. This will reposition the line hand so that another haul can be made on the forward cast.

Once the haul is made, let the imaginary rubber band pull your left hand back to the reel. Channel any slack line at your feet through the first guide. Don't let go of the line yet after the front haul. Controlling the slack between the line hand and the first guide is key. Practice double hauling until you can haul and maintain line-hand tension on both the front and back hauls (see illustration on page 97).

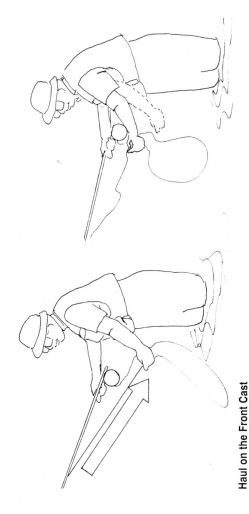

Haul on the Front Cast

The haul on the front cast is made at the same time the casting hand applies the power stroke. Practice repositioning the line hand even on the front haul, as this will help you control slack in the line.

97

Once you have control of the line on both hauls, try shooting more line on the front cast after you make the forward haul. Simply release the line with your left hand immediately after the forward haul is made. The line will fly out impressively if your timing and technique are sound. With proper timing and careful coiling of slack line at your feet, you can learn to shoot 30 feet of line or more by using the double haul. To maintain control of this shooting line, many casters use a stripping basket. These devices keep the line from tangling on itself or your shoelaces.

Shooting Line after the Forward Haul
Release line with your line hand right after the forward haul is made.

The double haul practice drill on grass.

Practice Drill: The Horizontal Double Haul

Find a grass lawn to practice this drill. Lower the casting plane so that the rod is horizontal to the ground, or so that you are casting completely side-arm.

Make a backcast with a haul and have the line hand follow back up to the reel. Let the line fall onto the grass after the cast is made.

Next, make a front cast with a haul and maintain line-hand tension so that the left hand bounces back to the reel.

Separate the backcast from the front cast and let the line fall on the ground after each cast. Watch as your hands start together and pull apart, with the left (line) hand then drifting back to the reel. This drill will help you learn to reposition your left hand and control line-hand tension.

Casting Drift

All accomplished fly casters naturally develop what is called a drift at the finish of each cast. This drift move is really just a smooth follow-through at the finish of the cast. Drifting allows the casting arc to expand while still having an abrupt stopping point in the stroke. Incorporating a drifting move will allow you to cast longer lines more gracefully, with less effort.

For the most part, there is little or no follow-through when you are casting shorter distances. Longer casts require an expanded casting arc to accommodate more line traveling through the air, so a longer follow-through is used when casting longer lines. The rod tip is still brought to a crisp stop, and the drift helps the casting arc expand after the stop.

At the Orvis schools, we address rod drifting only when a student demonstrates that he or she can cast a longer line effectively and can control the size of the casting arc to correspond with the amount of line being handled. Most people develop this drifting move naturally, but it is helpful to make them aware of their follow-through. Consciously drifting the rod at the finish of the stroke allows you to make smoother, more elaborate casts (see illustration).

1: Only a short drift is needed on short casts.

2: A longer drift is needed to help expand the casting arc on long casts.

CHAPTER 11

CASTING IN WINDY CONDITIONS

Casting a fly line is difficult when it's breezy and nearly impossible when the wind is blowing and gusting. Unfortunately, the wind is usually blowing to some degree when you are fishing. There are many ways to combat its effects, and in some situations you can use the wind to your advantage.

The most important skill to master when casting in windy conditions is controlling the size of your casting loop. Remember that narrow, well-defined casting loops travel and cut through the air more efficiently. Open or wide casting loops are less defined and are very ineffective at penetrating the wind.

Narrow loops are more aerodynamic than open loops because they transmit energy over a smaller radius. This smaller radius has less area exposed to the wind. Look at this another way: Which could you throw farther into a stiff breeze, a golf ball or a basketball? The golf ball has less surface area to be affected by the wind.

CASTING INTO A HEAD WIND

Casting directly into a head wind can be somewhat intimidating. However, casting into a head wind will assist the formation of the backcast, which can in turn benefit the forward cast. Personally, I find it easier to cast into a head wind than a tail wind.

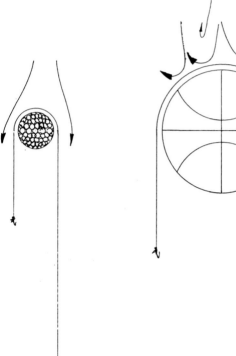

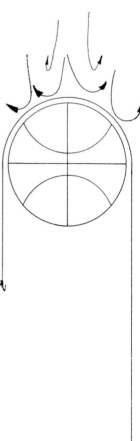

Tight Loops versus Open Loops

Which could you throw farther into a stiff wind, a golf ball or a basketball? Certainly the golf

When the wind is blowing right at you, your casting motion must change so there is little hang time once the line has been delivered. If the rod tip is stopped high, at eye level, the line will unfurl well above the surface of the water. Fly line is not very heavy, and it will blow erratically, like a leaf in the wind, if presented high above the water. Avoid this by driving the line lower over the water. This eliminates unnecessary hang time and the cast will find its mark.

You do this by lowering the rod tip at the finish of the front stroke. It's also helpful to shorten the backcast. The entire casting arc is tilted forward: The backcast stops almost vertically and the front stroke ends up near waist level or even lower. Try to imagine casting the line directly onto the surface of the water. Use the rod as a knife to cut down through a head wind (see illustration on page 106).

CASTING IN TAIL WINDS

Tail winds are cumbersome to fish in because they impede the formation of the backcast loop. If the wind is keeping the line from extending behind you, it makes presenting the fly forward extremely difficult. The trick is to do just the opposite of what you do when casting into a head wind: The casting arc should tilt backward slightly, so that the line will cut down through the wind on the backcast. On the forward stroke, stop the rod tip at a higher point than normal and let the breeze help carry the line forward. If you can cast the line under the wind behind you, a blowing

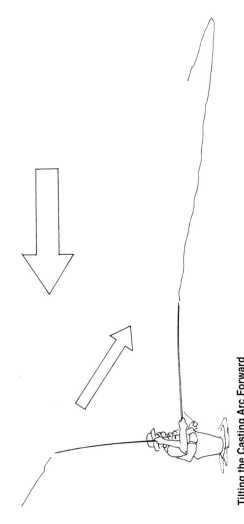

Tilting the Casting Arc Forward
To cast under a head wind, shorten your backcast and drive the rod tip to waist level on the front cast.

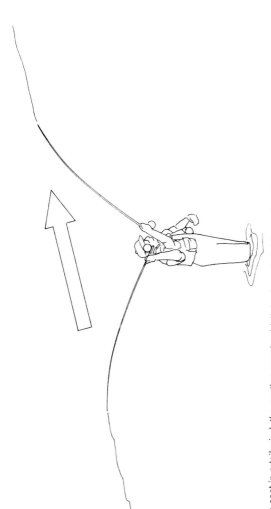

To cast in a tail wind, the casting arc should tilt backward slightly, so that the line will cut down through the wind on the backcast. On the forward stroke, stop the rod tip at a higher point than normal and let the wind help carry the line forward. This is not advised for beginners.

tail wind can really help lay the line out on the forward stroke (see illustration on page 107).

THE BELGIUM CAST

The Belgium cast is an excellent cast to use when the wind is at your back. On this cast, the line is pulled side-arm on the back stroke but is presented more overhead on the forward cast. You are actually changing casting planes. By adjusting the plane to a side-arm move on the back stroke, you can sneak the line under the wind behind you. Then just sweep the rod tip up overhead and cast the line forward as usual (see illustration).

SIDE-ARM CASTING

If the wind is unpredictable and gusting in all kinds of directions, it is often helpful to use side-arm casts. Angling the casting plane to the side will often let you cast under the wind. This can be helpful in many fishing situations. When saltwater fishing off a skiff in the flats, there are no barriers to block a strong breeze. Often the guide will rotate the boat at the last second to set up the best angle for you to cast at oncoming fish. If the wind is swirling, it is hard to tell which way the boat will be angled at the moment a cast needs to be made. Casting side-arm helps you get under the wind no matter what direction you're facing and allows you to present the fly. Tilting the rod to the side also puts the fly farther away from you, which will prevent it from hooking you as the cast is being made.

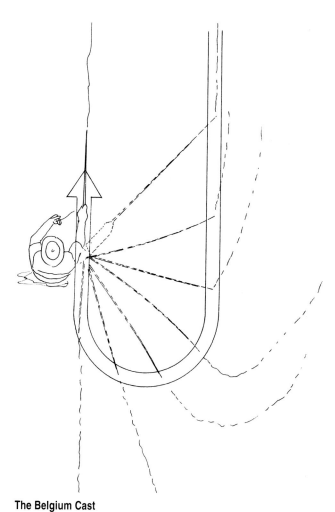

The Belgium Cast
On this overhead view, you can see that the backcast is made side-arm, but that the front cast is made more overhead. You are actually changing planes in the middle of the cast.

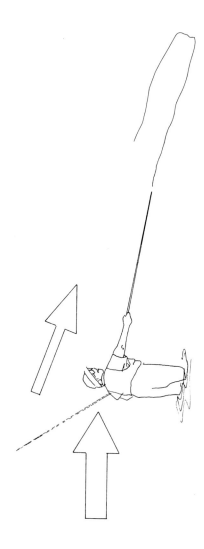

Backcast Presentation
In a cross wind that is blowing the line toward you, turn your back to the wind and present the fly on the backcast.

CROSS WINDS

When the wind is blowing across from right to left and you are casting with your right hand, the wind is pushing the line and fly into you. This makes casting difficult, because the hook will be whizzing near your head as you false cast the line. This type of right-to-left breeze is called a left-hander's wind, because the line and fly are pushed away from a lefty. (A wind blowing to the right is said to be a right-hander's wind.) Years ago an old striper fisherman in Rhode Island taught me to turn my line-hand shoulder to the wind and present the line on the backcast (see illustration on page 110). He instructed me to use the backcast as the presentation cast. This is particularly useful when the wind is gusting crossways. The wind will help blow the line and hook away from you or your rod tip.

Delivering the line on the back stroke has it limitations. It is difficult to be accurate in the tight quarters of a small stream when you are dry-fly fishing, for example. However, this technique is ideal for saltwater fishing in open spaces.

CHAPTER 12

PRESENTATION CASTS

SLACK-LINE CASTS

Many situations call for the line to extend out perfectly toward the fish. Hitting the mark with your fly is the goal—but as the fly moves through the water, the way it drifts or floats is often the real reason why a fish decides to take your offering. Most of a trout's diet floats naturally in the current, for example. A straight-line cast is ideal for presenting the fly to the target, but will sometimes cause the fly to drag artificially through the water. To counter this, you often need to add some slack into the cast, so the fly drifts naturally once it lands in the current. Slack-line casts will enhance your presentation with the fly rod, so add them to your casting repertoire.

The Reach Cast

Fishing in rivers and streams can be difficult when cross currents disturb the natural drift of the fly. The reach cast, or reach-mend cast, is used to deliver line across a stream with different current speeds. Before the line falls on to the swirling currents, the rod tip is pushed or flipped upstream so that some slack line falls onto the water. This allows the fly to drift drag free. Make an overhead cast and wait until the line completely unfurls in the air. Now swing the rod tip

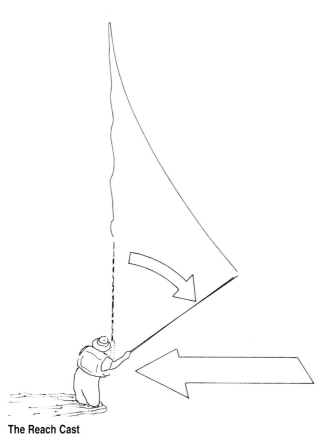

The Reach Cast
Before the line falls on to swirling currents, the rod tip is pushed or flipped upstream so that some slack line is added to the cast. This slack will allow the fly to drift drag free.

upcurrent and let some slack form near the rod tip as the line falls to the water. This will reposition the line across the stream, but the slack line will be above the fly. As the fly drifts downstream, the slack line will be in the faster current, allowing the fly to be undisturbed as it is presented to the fish. The reach cast permits longer, drag-free drifts that can produce fish when dealing with tricky cross-stream presentations.

The S-Cast

The S-cast is used to add slack into the line as it is presented to the water, allowing the fly to drift realistically in the current. As the cast is delivered, the rod tip is wiggled back and forth before the line falls onto the water. These S curves provide slack in the line as it drifts over multiple currents. The S-cast is easy to do, but the trick is to add the S curves after you complete your normal forward cast. Finish the forward stroke, stop the rod tip at around eye level, then wiggle the rod tip side to side, putting some S curves in the line as it falls to the water. You can put a few big S curves or a bunch of smaller ones, depending on the situation. If you are fishing on a small trout stream with tiny micro-currents, a few small S curves are all you need to eliminate drag on your fly. On larger, more turbulent rivers you may need to make more S curves with larger loops. The way you shake the rod tip at the end of the cast will determine the size and number of S curves you put in the line (see illustration).

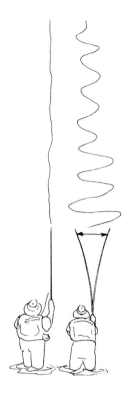

The S-Cast
To get a drag-free float over multiple currents, wriggle the rod tip back and forth. These S curves provide slack so the fly can drift drag free over multiple currents.

The Fly-First or Tuck Cast

The fly-first cast is used in many fishing situations, and is a way to present the fly on the water ahead of the line. This cast may be used to drive a subsurface fly into the water so that it sinks quickly. It can also be effective when you're fishing pocket water with dry flies. This cast lets you be very precise at dropping a dry fly tightly into the quiet water behind rocks or other obstructions. Because the fly lands on the water first, it will give you a few valuable moments of drag-free drift before the line lands on the water.

To present the fly first, your front cast needs to be slightly overpowered or accelerated to a high and aggressive stop. Make a normal high backcast, then drive the rod tip to an abrupt stop on the front cast. Stop the rod tip high overhead, above eye level. The combination of overpowering the front stroke and stopping the tip higher will force the fly to hit the water ahead of the line (see illustration).

The Curve Cast

The curve cast is really just a tuck or a fly-first cast turned on its side. The fly-first cast is executed vertically; the curve cast is the same motion, just angled more horizontally. Rather than overpowering the rod to a stop high overhead, lower the casting plane more to the side and cast the fly around a corner. The more you drop the cast on its side, the more the fly will swing around a curve. The key is to not let the rod tip lag around to a slow stop at finish. Drive the front

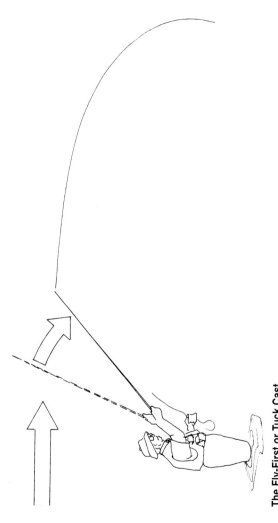

The Fly-First or Tuck Cast
The combination of slightly overpowering the front cast and stopping the rod tip at a higher point in the arc will force the fly to hit the water ahead of the line.

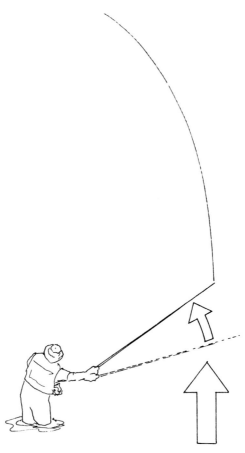

Curve Cast

A curve cast is really a tuck cast thrown side-arm. Lower your casting plane so you are almost casting side-arm. Energetically bring the rod to a stop, and the extra line speed will sling the line around a corner.

stroke side-arm to a hard stop and cast the line around a corner. The line will go in whatever direction the tip points when it is accelerated to a stop.

This cast is very useful for presenting a fly under overhanging trees or branches, especially to hard-to-catch fish. As trout see more and more flies, they become increasingly leader-shy. The curve cast is popular because a fly can be cast upstream and curved around and over to a feeding fish. This way the line and leader do not drift over a fish's head.

THE PARACHUTE CAST

Downstream presentations can be very effective at fooling wise old trout. When you're casting downstream, the fish will see the fly first, not the leader or line. If you position yourself effectively upstream, a downstream presentation can make a difference when casting to leader-shy fish.

The parachute cast is most often used when casting downstream to feeding fish. If a straight-line cast is made downstream, the fly will drag as it hits the water. With the parachute cast, the rod tip is stopped at a high point in the arc, so the fly will land softly upstream, above the fish. As the fly touches the water, the rod tip is lowered at the same pace as the river's flow. This way the fly drifts naturally downstream to the target. This is an excellent way to present flies downstream, and you won't miss strikes, because there is very little slack in the line as the rod tip is lowered downriver. The key is to make sure that the rod is lowered at the

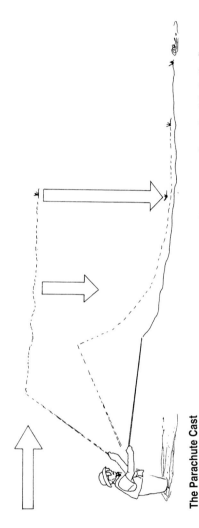

The Parachute Cast
On this cast the rod tip stopped high overhead so the fly lands softly upstream, above the fish. As the fly touches the water, the rod is lowered so that the fly drifts at the same pace of the river's flow.

same rate as the river's flow. If it is lowered too slowly, the fly will drag.

The S-cast is also used for downstream presentations, but the slack created with this cast makes it hard to set the hook when the fish takes the fly. When using the parachute cast, the slack line can be controlled as the rod tip and line is lowered quietly to the fish.

TROUBLESHOOTING

1. **Problem:** When double hauling, slack forms between the line hand and the stripping guide after the back haul, and there is no line tension available to perform the forward haul.
   - **Cause:** The back or first haul is too aggressive and too much line has been pulled on the back haul. Pulling excessively on the back haul creates slack between the stripping guide and the line hand.
   - **Solution:** Make a short, crisp back haul so that there is less line to take up on the repositioning of the line hand for the forward haul. Don't rip the line out on the back haul so that your hands are pulled wildly apart. Your hands should never be more than 24 to 30 inches apart when attempting to double haul.

   Tip: When attempting to learn the double haul, it is easier with heavier line weights. Smaller, delicate trout rods (4-weight or less) are difficult because the lines are so light that it is hard to maintain line tension while double hauling. Instead, try the double haul with a 7- or 8-weight. Better yet, try a shooting head! These heavier lines will suck up the slack effectively on the back haul, making it easier to reposition the line hand back to the reel before the forward haul.

2. **Problem:** Tailing loops form when double hauling.
   - **Cause:** The timing of the hauls is off. The line is being pulled or hauled prematurely during the casting stroke. The haul is being made before the casting stroke is executed, in other words.
   - **Solution:** The hauls need to be smoothly timed with the power stroke. Make a short, crisp tug on the line as the power stroke is applied.

CHAPTER 13

CONCLUSION

No one is born with a graceful and effortless fly-casting stroke. Most expert fly casters earned their stripes by refining their techniques on the practice pond. Fly casting is a sport, and if you want to be good at it, you need to practice. For every 7 iron a golfer hits within two feet of the flag, there are countless balls hit at the driving range. When a 20-inch brown trout is sipping midges in a tight spot on the river and your presentation needs to be perfect, this is no time for a practice cast. So set aside some time to improve your fly casting when you're not fishing.

Develop a simple practice routine that you can stick with. I recommend 20-minute sessions a few times a week. This does not eat up too much time and it can fit into the busiest of schedules. If you are just getting started, avoid long practice sessions. I prefer short but regular casting sessions. This will promote positive muscle memory. Longer practice sessions tend to be counterproductive; bad habits may creep in as the casting arm tires.

If you really want to become a better fly caster, reading this book is a good start. However, the best way to improve your skills is to take lessons from a qualified instructor or to attend an established fly-fishing school. Proper instruction will speed up your learning curve dramatically. Best of luck to you!

And here's what it's all about—a large brown trout. You won't catch a trout like this without the casting accuracy that comes from practice.

GLOSSARY

Butt section: The bottom section of a fly rod that is attached to the cork grip.

Casting arc: The distance the rod travels through a fly casting stroke.

Casting drift: Drift is the follow-through component of fly casting. It is what allows the casting arc to expand, while still having abrupt stopping points.

Casting hand: The hand in which you hold the rod grip.

Casting loop: An open-ended loop that unfurls or unrolls off the end of the rod tip. This can be on the backcast or front cast.

Casting plane: The angle at which the fly-casting stroke is made. For example, the stroke can be side-arm or overhead or somewhere in between.

Double haul: The act of pulling on the line during the power stroke on both the backcast and forwardcast.

False casting: The act of holding the line aloft with a series of back and forth casts, where the line does not touch the water below.

Leader: A tapered piece of monofilament that serves as the invisible link between fly line and fly. Average length is nine feet.

Line hand: The opposite of the hand that is holding the rod grip. If you hold the rod and cast with your right hand, your line hand would be your left.

Pick-up and lay-down cast: The most basic cast made by simply picking up the line with a backcast stroke, then laying it back down with a front cast.

Power stroke: The point in the cast when the forearm and wrist apply acceleration. This is performed near the end of the cast and followed by the rod stopping abruptly. Synonyms: speed up and stop, power snap, wrist snap.

Presentation: The act of laying the line on the water to an intended target.

Rod tip: The top section of a fly rod.

Roll cast: A cast where no backcast is needed and the end of the fly line is anchored in the water, then rolled out over the water.

Shooting line: The act of releasing the line with the line hand at the completion of a cast.

Single haul: The act of pulling on the line with the non-casting hand during the power stroke on either the backcast or front cast.

Slack line: Line between the line hand and rod that is not under tension during the act of fly casting. It is also the line that dangles below the casting hand and the reel that is prepared for shooting.

Tippet: The end section of a leader where the fly is attached. It is most often the smallest diameter and the weakest link of a leader.

Tailing loop: When the line or leader runs into itself or the loop is closed during the cast. This will sometimes produce knots in the end of the leader.

Wind knot: An overhand or other type of knot formed in the leader that is caused by casting error or windy conditions.

INDEX